Prosecco
COCKTAILS

Senior Designer Barbara Zuñiga
Text Editor Lesley Malkin
Production Manager Gordana Simakovic
Editorial Director Julia Charles
Art Director Leslie Harrington
Publisher Cindy Richards

Drinks Stylist Lorna Brash
Prop Stylist Luis Peral
Indexer Hilary Bird

First published in 2017 by
Ryland Peters & Small
20—21 Jockey's Fields
London WC1R 4BW
and
341 E 116th Street
New York, 10029
www.rylandpeters.com

10 9 8 7 6 5 4

ISBN: 978-1-84975-895-6

A CIP record for this book is available from
the British Library. US Library of Congress CIP
data has been applied for.

Printed in China

Acknowledgements
The author and the publishers would like
to thank Popaball® for kindly providing
the Popaball Bursting Bubbles used in the
cocktails featured on pages 35, 43, 47, 48, 52
and 56. Visit www.popaball.co.uk for more
information about the full product range.

With thanks to Niall Kishtainy for
being an excellent cocktail wingman

Prosecco
COCKTAILS

40 tantalizing recipes
for everyone's favourite sparkler

Laura Gladwin

photography by Alex Luck

RYLAND PETERS & SMALL
LONDON • NEW YORK

Contents

Prosecco Power

Ah, Prosecco, how we love it! Italy's most affable sparkling wine has long since overtaken Champagne in popularity, and our thirst for it shows no sign of abating. Light, fresh, fruity and uncomplicated, Prosecco's sprightly bubbles go with just about anything, as its fans are keen to demonstrate. But why serve it on its own when there are so many things you could add to make it even lovelier? Now it's time to fully embrace Prosecco's cocktail potential. What many of us don't realize is that those easy-drinking qualities we love so much are exactly what makes it a great base for cocktails. Prosecco is perfect for adding an extra dose of festive sparkle to your next shindig: whether it's a special birthday or a girls' night in; an action-packed hen party or a dainty baby shower; a sunny beachside barbecue or an intimate meal *à deux*; a fun family celebration or an elegant dinner party, a Prosecco cocktail will add celebratory sparkle to any occasion.

Prosecco + cocktails = a match made in heaven

Prosecco is made from the Glera grape, which finds its natural home in the gently rolling hills of the Veneto region, north of Venice. Since 2009, Italian wine regulations have meant that only wine from this particular region can be labelled as Prosecco. It's made in a similar way to Champagne, with natural bubbles, but the main fermentation takes place in large tanks rather than in the bottle, which makes it more cost-effective to produce – so plenty more lovely bubbles for us! Its natural, clean flavours, which wine experts often say are reminiscent of apples and pears, partner perfectly with all kinds of spirits, and can take stronger fruity flavours too. The addition of Prosecco both lightens and adds body to all manner of classic cocktails, as well as lending itself to fresh new concoctions.

Prosecco cocktail know-how

To make great Prosecco cocktails you don't need any fancy equipment – just a cocktail shaker, some attractive glassware and plenty of ice. As with any cocktail, the key to making a good one is keeping everything as cold as possible. For the recipes in this book you need a standard, dry Prosecco – just make sure it's really well chilled. If you forgot to put it in the fridge, never fear! A quick tip for chilling it quickly is to wrap it in wet kitchen towel and put it in the freezer.

Brunch Cocktails

La Passeggiata

The *passeggiata* is an excellent Italian tradition of taking an evening stroll along a scenic boulevard, dressed up to the nines, to check out your neighbours. Why not give it a try down your road after breakfast, accompanied by one of these?

75 ml/3 oz chilled pink grapefruit juice
20 ml/¾ oz gin
20 ml/¾ oz Aperol
well-chilled Prosecco, to top
strip of grapefruit zest, to garnish (optional)
MAKES 1

Half-fill a collins glass with ice cubes. Add the pink grapefruit juice, gin and Aperol and stir well. Top with Prosecco and stir very briefly. If you like, squeeze a strip of grapefruit zest over the top and drop it in.

Mimosa

Presenting the Bucks Fizz's much classier cousin from across the pond: the Mimosa, which is beautifully enhanced by a dash of Cointreau.

about 65 ml/2¾ oz well-chilled freshly squeezed orange juice

1 teaspoon Cointreau

about 65 ml/2¾ oz well-chilled Prosecco

MAKES 1

Half-fill a cold champagne flute with the orange juice. Add the Cointreau and half the Prosecco. Stir gently, then add the rest and serve immediately.

NOTE: if you're making a trayful, help the bubbles stay perky by adding half the Prosecco and stirring all the glasses. Finish off with the final dose of Prosecco just before serving.

Bellini

Mmmm, the golden sunlight of a palazzo terrace on the Grand Canal in Venice, ice-cold Bellini in hand... If you're a bit short on Italian glamour, never mind – just serve a round of these at your next soirée.

35 ml/1½ oz good-quality, well-chilled peach juice

a dash of Chambord (optional; worth it though for its beautiful rosy blush)

well-chilled Prosecco, to top

MAKES 1

Pour the peach juice into a cold champagne flute and stir in the Chambord, if using. Half-fill with Prosecco and stir gently. Add the rest and serve.

Prosecco Mary

Think of the Prosecco Mary as the Bloody Mary's younger and slightly more glamorous sister (if the mere thought doesn't make you shudder...)

25 ml/1 oz vodka
75 ml/3 oz tomato juice
dash of Tabasco or sriracha
pinch of sugar
dash of smoked water
(optional; available in some supermarkets, and fun!)
about 75 ml/3 oz Prosecco
cucumber slices and/or a celery stick, to garnish
MAKES 1

Put the vodka, tomato juice, Tabasco, sugar and smoked water, if using, into a cocktail shaker half-filled with ice cubes. Shake vigorously and pour, ice cubes and all, into a chilled collins glass.

Add half the Prosecco and stir gently to combine. Top with the rest of the Prosecco, add some cucumber slices down the side of the glass (or a celery stick if you prefer) and serve with straw and stirrer.

NOTE: Smoked water is delicious but can overpower, so exercise caution and use no more than ¼ teaspoon to begin with.

La Dolce Vita

They don't call this delicious cocktail *la dolce vita* ('the good life') for nothing. It's a brilliantly fresh and light brunch accompaniment if you want something a bit different.

seedless white grapes
1 teaspoon honey
25 ml/1 oz vodka
well-chilled Prosecco, to top

MAKES 1

Put five of the grapes (keep a small cluster in reserve for garnish, if liked) in a cocktail shaker with the honey and muddle well until they release their juice. Add the vodka and half-fill the shaker with ice cubes. Shake vigorously, then strain into a cold martini glass. Top with Prosecco and serve immediately.

Breakfast in Milan

OK, so you don't have to wake up in Milan, but you'll definitely feel a lot more chic after getting one of these down you, along with a melt-in-the-mouth pastry. Continental breakfast in bed, anyone?

3 teaspoons shredless orange marmalade
15 ml/½ oz freshly squeezed lime juice
dash of Campari (optional)
25 ml/1 oz gin
well-chilled Prosecco, to top
MAKES 1

Put the marmalade in a cocktail shaker with the lime juice, Campari, if using, and gin. Half-fill the shaker with ice cubes and shake vigorously. Strain into a cold martini glass and top with Prosecco. Serve immediately.

Aperitivi

The Perfect Spritz

Ignore what it says on the side of your Aperol bottle and make
your spritz this way instead. The Italians knew what they were
doing when they came up with this one.

35 ml/1½ oz Aperol
75 ml/3 oz well-chilled Prosecco
soda water, to top
orange slice, to garnish
MAKES 1

Half-fill a large wine glass or collins glass with ice cubes. Pour in the
Aperol and half the Prosecco and stir gently. Add the rest of the Prosecco,
top with a splash of soda and add the orange slice. Serve immediately.

Prosecco Classico

If it's good enough for Champagne, it's good enough for Prosecco!
Roll out the red carpet and give yours the Hollywood star treatment
by serving it in classic sparkling cocktail style.

Angostura bitters
1 sugar cube
dash of brandy (optional)

125 ml/4½ oz well-chilled
Prosecco

MAKES 1

Drop several dashes of Angostura bitters onto the sugar cube and put it
in a chilled Champagne flute. Add a dash of brandy, if using, then add the
Prosecco and serve immediately.

Prosecco White Lady

A cocktail legend made even lovelier, thanks to a generous helping
of Prosecco. The White Lady is a slinky, sophisticated 1920s classic
– and so will you be once you've sipped one of these!

35 ml/1½ oz gin
15 ml/½ oz Cointreau
well-chilled Prosecco, to top

15 ml/½ oz freshly squeezed
lemon juice

MAKES 1

Pour the gin and Cointreau into a cocktail shaker half-filled with ice
cubes. Stir until very cold, then strain into a chilled martini glass. Top with
Prosecco and the lemon juice and serve immediately.

Beretta 18

Another Italian take on a classic, the French 75. Both are named after World War I artillery and both are classy numbers — serve up one of these and you're bound to impress your guests.

25 ml/1 oz gin
15 ml/½ oz limoncello
well-chilled Prosecco, to top
strip of lemon zest, to garnish
MAKES 1

Put the gin and limoncello in a cocktail shaker or collins glass with a handful of ice cubes and stir until they are very cold. Strain into a chilled Champagne flute and top with Prosecco. Squeeze the lemon zest in half lengthways over the drink so that the essential oils in the skin spritz over it, then drop it in and serve immediately.

Bridge of Sighs

This was named after the famous enclosed bridge in Venice, under which, legend has it, lovers will be granted eternal bliss if they kiss on a gondola at sunset. It might be easier to just drink one of these, and sigh with bliss...

caster/superfine sugar, to decorate the glass (optional)
15 ml/½ oz gin
15 ml/½ oz elderflower liqueur
well-chilled Prosecco, to top
MAKES 1

If you like, moisten the rim of a chilled Champagne flute with water and dip it into a saucer filled with caster sugar to create a rim around the glass. Put the gin and elderflower liqueur in a cocktail shaker with a handful of ice cubes and stir. Strain carefully into the flute. Add half the Prosecco and stir gently, then add the rest and serve immediately.

Kir Reali

The French have their Kir Royale (sparkling wine with crème de cassis, also nice with Prosecco), and the Kir Reali is the Italian version. All together now: *When the moon hits your eye like a big pizza pie, that's amore…*

10 ml/⅓ oz crème de violette

125 ml/4½ oz well-chilled Prosecco

strip of lemon zest, to garnish

MAKES 1

Pour the crème de violette into a chilled Champagne flute and add the Prosecco. Squeeze the lemon zest in half lengthways over the drink so that the essential oils in the skin spritz over it, then drop it in and serve immediately.

Chaise Longue

This is based on a classic cocktail invented by Ernest Hemingway, Death in the Afternoon, but is tempered by the decidedly un-Hemingway-like addition of rose water. He would have added twice as much absinthe, but even as it is you might be glad of a lie down on a chaise longue after drinking one!

15 ml/½ oz absinthe (preferably pre-chilled in the fridge)

dash of rose water

125 ml/4½ oz well-chilled Prosecco

MAKES 1

Pour the absinthe into a chilled Champagne flute and add a dash of rose water. Gently pour over the Prosecco and serve.

Sbagliato

No need to worry about your hand 'slipping' with the gin here – *sbagliato* means 'mistaken', and this is a rough-and-ready, but rather delicious version, of the chic Negroni cocktail.

25 ml/1 oz red Italian vermouth
25 ml/1 oz Campari

75 ml/3 oz well-chilled Prosecco

MAKES 1

Fill an old-fashioned glass with ice and add the vermouth and Campari. Stir well. Add the Prosecco and stir very gently to preserve the fizz. Serve immediately.

Tiziano

This gorgeous red concoction would be just perfect to kick off an intimate meal *à deux*. Dubonnet's Rouge Aperitif wine has been a staple on the cocktail landscape since 1846, and rightly so!

10 red grapes
75 ml/3 oz Dubonnet
well-chilled Prosecco, to top

strip of orange zest, to garnish

MAKES 1

Put nine of the grapes into a cocktail shaker and muddle them to crush and extract the juice. Add a handful of ice cubes and the Dubonnet and shake vigorously. Strain into an old-fashioned glass, add some ice and top with Prosecco. Squeeze the zest lengthways to spritz the essential oils in the skin over the drink. Garnish with it and the remaining grape on a cocktail stick.

Bello Marcello

Even the most committed whisky-phobe will love this one.
There's no better use for Grandad's treasured single malt!

35 ml/1½ oz whisky
15 ml/½ oz Cointreau
well-chilled Prosecco, to top
strip of lemon zest, to garnish

MAKES 1

Pour the whisky and Cointreau into an old-fashioned glass filled with
ice. Stir well, then top up with Prosecco. Squeeze the lemon zest in
half lengthways over the drink so that the essential oils in the skin
spritz over it, then serve.

Summer Coolers

Pimm's Deluxe

Once you've tried this you'll wonder why you haven't been adding Prosecco to Pimm's all your life — it's a knockout. Although it is best to keep in mind that it packs more of a punch than your regular Pimm's and lemonade!

50 ml/2 oz Pimm's
dash of elderflower cordial
sliced strawberries, orange, lemon and cucumber
well-chilled Prosecco, to top
a sprig of mint
MAKES 1

Fill a collins glass with ice cubes and add the Pimm's, elderflower and sliced fruit. Stir well, then half-fill with Prosecco. Stir gently, then add the rest of the Prosecco. Lightly crush the mint sprig and drop it in the top.

NOTE: if serving lots of people, make a pitcher of this ahead of time, which helps extract more flavour from the fruit, adding the ice, Prosecco and mint just before serving. For a 2-litre/2-quart pitcher, use 750 ml/26 oz Prosecco, 400 ml/ 14 oz Pimms and 50 ml/2 oz elderflower cordial.

Sangria Blanca

This peachy little number will get the fiesta started. Get out all your best cocktail 'furniture': this is no time to be tasteful.

¼ ripe peach or nectarine, skin on

10 ml/¼ oz freshly squeezed lemon juice

25 ml/1 oz golden rum

15 ml/½ oz peach schnapps

25 ml/1 oz peach juice

well-chilled Prosecco, to top

MAKES 1

Thinly slice the peach and put it with the lemon juice, rum, peach schnapps and peach juice into a collins glass and stir well. Add a handful of ice cubes and top with Prosecco. Stir very gently, add your adornments and serve.

La Rossa

Summer in a glass. All you need is a picnic blanket, a secluded meadow and someone rather lovely to snuggle up to.

4 strawberries

1 teaspoon sugar

25 ml/1 oz limoncello

1 teaspoon strawberry bursting bubbles (optional), see page 2

well-chilled Prosecco, to top

MAKES 1

Hull three of the strawberries and chop them. Put in a cocktail shaker with the sugar and muddle until the juices are released. Add the limoncello, half-fill the shaker with ice cubes and shake. Strain into a chilled Champagne flute. Add the bursting bubbles, if using. Half-fill the glass with Prosecco, stir, and then top up. Slice the remaining strawberry and use it to garnish.

Prosecco Iced Tea

Tea, gin and Prosecco: all your favourite refreshments in one glass! Heaven. Next time you fancy a Long Island Iced Tea, think again, and try this far more elegant concoction instead.

1 Earl Grey tea bag

1 tablespoon sugar

25 ml/1 oz gin

1 teaspoon freshly squeezed lemon juice

dash of elderflower cordial

well-chilled Prosecco, to top

lemon slices, to garnish

MAKES 1

First, make an infusion by putting the tea bag and sugar in a mug and pouring over 75 ml/3 oz boiling water, then leave for 5 minutes. Remove the tea bag and leave to cool to room temperature.

Pour the Earl Grey infusion into a collins glass and add the gin, lemon juice and elderflower cordial. Half-fill with ice cubes and stir well. Top with Prosecco and garnish with a couple of lemon slices, and a straw if you like.

Hugo

Who's Hugo? His identity remains a mystery, but he came up with a damn fine drink. Let's imagine he's a suave, chisel-jawed man-about-town who created this ravishing elderflower concoction just for you…

6 mint leaves

¼ lime, cut into wedges

25 ml/1 oz elderflower cordial

well-chilled Prosecco, to top

splash of soda water

MAKES 1

Put four of the mint leaves and the lime wedges in a balloon glass and muddle them lightly. Add the elderflower cordial, a handful of ice cubes and half-fill with Prosecco. Stir gently. Top up with Prosecco and a splash of soda water and garnish with the remaining mint leaves. Serve with a straw.

Nonna's Garden

The gorgeous combination of cucumber and mint smells fresh and light — just like the beautiful garden Grandma spends so long weeding! You can also try fresh basil or sage leaves instead of the mint.

3 large slices of cucumber, plus 1 small slice to garnish

1 teaspoon freshly squeezed lemon juice

1 teaspoon sugar

5 mint leaves

well-chilled Prosecco, to top

MAKES 1

Put the cucumber, lemon juice, sugar and four of the mint leaves into a cocktail shaker and muddle well. Half-fill the shaker with ice cubes and shake vigorously. Strain into a chilled balloon glass and top with Prosecco. Garnish with a mint leaf and a slice of cucumber.

Hibiscus Fizz

Hibiscus flowers are said to have health benefits, but never mind all that, let's put some in Prosecco! The flowers preserved in syrup are widely available now, and add a lovely pink colour and sweet, fruity tang to your bubbles. Couldn't be easier or prettier.

1 hibiscus flower in syrup
dash of Chambord or crème de framboise (optional)
well-chilled Prosecco, to top
MAKES 1

Carefully place the hibiscus flower with the petals facing upwards in the bottom of a chilled Champagne flute. Add the Chambord, if using. Slowly pour in the Prosecco and serve.

Rosebud

Feisty yet delicate, and strangely captivating… no, not a plucky romantic heroine, but a rather lovely summer cooler.

1 teaspoon rose water
20 ml/¾ oz elderflower liqueur
15 ml/½ oz gin
1 teaspoon freshly squeezed lemon juice

well-chilled Prosecco, to top
edible rose petal, to garnish (optional)

MAKES 1

Put the rose water, elderflower liqueur, gin and lemon juice in a cocktail shaker. Add a handful of ice and shake well. Strain into a chilled Champagne flute and top with Prosecco. Garnish with a rose petal and serve immediately.

Raspberry Dazzler

The thinking person's strawberry is shown off to best advantage in this delectably fruity and intense creation.

4 fresh raspberries
½ teaspoon sugar
1 teaspoon Chambord
25 ml/1 oz vodka

1 teaspoon raspberry bursting bubbles (optional), see page 2
well-chilled Prosecco, to top

MAKES 1

Put the raspberries and sugar in a cocktail shaker and muddle well. Add the Chambord and vodka and a handful of ice cubes and shake well. Strain into a chilled Champagne flute and add the bursting bubbles, if using. Add half the Prosecco, stir gently, then add the rest and serve immediately.

Sgroppino

Equally at home as a drink or as dessert, this is the most gorgeous slush puppy you've ever encountered.

25 ml/1 oz frozen vodka
1 generous tablespoon lemon sorbet
dash of egg white (optional)
well-chilled Prosecco, to top
finely sliced or grated lemon zest, to decorate

MAKES 1

If you have time, put the vodka and a small mixing bowl in the freezer for a few hours first. Put the vodka, sorbet, egg white, if using (it's a nice addition as it makes it more frothy), and half the Prosecco in the bowl and whisk well to combine.

Transfer to a chilled coupe or martini glass or a Champagne flute. Add the rest of the Prosecco and stir very gently. Scatter with strips of lemon zest and serve immediately. Add a spoon or a straw, depending on what is most practical with your choice of glassware.

Party Drinks

Prosecco Passion

Here's a simplified Prosecco twist on that absolute cocktail classic, the Porn Star. Serve with more Prosecco and bursting bubbles in a shot glass on the side, if you like.

25 ml/1 oz vodka
½ teaspoon vanilla paste or extract
1 teaspoon sugar
1 passion fruit
1 teaspoon passion fruit bursting bubbles (optional), see page 2
well-chilled Prosecco, to top
vanilla pod/bean, to garnish (optional)

MAKES 1

Put the vodka, vanilla and sugar in a cocktail shaker. Halve the passion fruit, scoop out all the flesh and seeds and drop them in the shaker. Add a handful of ice cubes and shake vigorously. Strain into a chilled martini glass and add the bursting bubbles, if using. Top with Prosecco and serve immediately, with a vanilla pod/bean stirrer to garnish, if you like.

Prosecco Cosmopolitan

You can bet that Carrie would have guzzled this in *Sex and the City* – THE classic girls' night out cocktail given extra pep with Prosecco!

25 ml/1 oz vodka
50 ml/2 oz cranberry juice
1 teaspoon freshly squeezed lime juice

well-chilled Prosecco, to top
strip of orange zest, to garnish

MAKES 1

Put the vodka, cranberry juice and lime juice in a cocktail shaker with a handful of ice cubes. Shake well and strain into a chilled martini glass. Top with Prosecco. Squeeze the orange zest strip in half lengthways so that the essential oils in the skin spritz on to the drink, then drop it in. Serve immediately.

Prima Donna

Let your inner diva enjoy this dazzling pomegranate and limoncello number! Quite a performance.

25 ml/1 oz vodka
15 ml/½ oz limoncello
25 ml/1 oz pomegranate juice

1 teaspoon lemon bursting bubbles (optional), see page 2
well-chilled Prosecco, to top

MAKES 1

Put the vodka, limoncello and pomegranate juice in a cocktail shaker and add a handful of ice cubes. Shake well and strain into a chilled Champagne flute. Add the bursting bubbles, if using, then top with Prosecco and serve.

Jalisco Flower

Lovers of tequila will be wowed by this classy combination, which adds up to so much more than the sum of its parts. *Arriba*!

15 ml/½ oz tequila
20 ml/¾ oz elderflower liqueur
35 ml/1½ oz pink grapefruit juice
well-chilled Prosecco, to top
edible flower, such as nasturtium or violet,
to garnish

MAKES 1

Put the tequila, elderflower liqueur and pink grapefruit juice in a cocktail shaker and add a handful of ice cubes. Shake well and strain into a chilled martini glass. Top with Prosecco and garnish with an edible flower.

Dark Forest

Dark, fruity, mysterious... No, I'm not talking about your next romantic assignation, but this delightful sparkler.

15 ml/½ oz Chambord
15 ml/½ oz crème de cassis
1 teaspoon blueberry bursting bubbles (optional), see page 2
well-chilled Prosecco, to top

MAKES 1

Put the Chambord and crème de cassis in a cocktail shaker with a handful of ice cubes and shake well. Strain into a chilled Champagne flute and add the bursting bubbles, if using. Top with Prosecco and serve immediately.

Blackberry Barfly

Dark and heady, with a deliciously unexpected tang of balsamic vinegar, this is a perfect late-night reviver.

5 blackberries
½ teaspoon balsamic vinegar
25 ml/1 oz sloe gin
well-chilled Prosecco, to top

MAKES 1

Put the blackberries in a cocktail shaker with the balsamic vinegar and crush with a muddler until they release all their juice. Add the sloe gin and a handful of crushed ice and shake well. Strain into an old-fashioned glass and top with Prosecco. Serve immediately.

Ultra Violet

Roses are red, but violets are *so* much more chic right now.
Try out this subtly floral delight at your next drinks party and
you'll be rewarded with plenty of *oohs* and *aahs*.

25 ml/1 oz gin
20 ml/¾ oz crème de violette
10 ml/¼ oz blue curaçao
10 ml/¼ oz freshly squeezed lemon juice
well-chilled Prosecco, to top
strip of lemon zest and an edible flower, to garnish
MAKES 1

Put the gin, crème de violette, blue curaçao and lemon juice in a cocktail
shaker and add a handful of ice cubes. Shake well, then strain into
a chilled martini glass. Top with Prosecco, garnish with lemon zest and an
edible flower. Serve immediately.

Cherry Baby

Bakewell tart in a glass, you say? Yes please! Lovers of cherry and almond cake everywhere will be delighted with this.

25 ml/1 oz Amaretto
15 ml/½ oz kirsch or cherry brandy
25 ml/1 oz cherry juice, or the syrup from a can of cherries

1 teaspoon cherry bursting bubbles (optional), see page 2
well-chilled Prosecco, to top

MAKES 1

Put the Amaretto, kirsch and cherry juice in a cocktail shaker and add a handful of ice cubes. Shake well, then strain into an old-fashioned glass. Add the bursting bubbles, if using, then top with Prosecco. Serve immediately.

Stiletto

This one's simple but delicious, and just like its namesake, adding one to your next soirée will definitely make an elegant fashion statement.

25 ml/1 oz Amaretto
15 ml/½ oz freshly squeezed lime juice

well-chilled Prosecco, to top
lime slice, to garnish

MAKES 1

Put the Amaretto and lime juice in a cocktail shaker with a handful of ice and shake well. Strain into a chilled Champagne coupe, add the Prosecco and garnish with a thin slice of lime. Serve immediately.

Airmail

Imagine you're sitting in the cocktail lounge on a luxury cruise, wearing Dior and white satin gloves with Rita Hayworth on the next table. This is almost certainly what you're drinking...

35 ml/1½ oz dark rum
15 ml/½ oz freshly squeezed lime juice
lime slice

10 ml/¼ oz honey mixed with 1 teaspoon boiling water
well-chilled Prosecco, to top

MAKES 1

Put the rum, lime juice and slice and honey in an old-fashioned glass, add a handful of ice cubes and stir. Top up with Prosecco and serve.

Prosecco Mojito

Everything you love about the mojito, with a dash of Prosecco in the mix instead of soda water (pah!) to liven up proceedings.

10 mint leaves, plus extra to garnish
1 teaspoon sugar
½ lime, cut into wedges

35 ml/1½ oz white rum
well-chilled Prosecco, to top

MAKES 1

Put the mint leaves, sugar and lime wedges in a collins glass and muddle well. Add the rum, stir and fill the glass with crushed ice. Top with Prosecco and stir very gently. Serve with more lightly crushed mint leaves.

Night Owl

Any night owl worth their salt, and even a few who should know better, will enjoy this wickedly quaffable creation.

15 ml/½ oz gin
15 ml/½ oz crème de cassis
15 ml/½ oz pomegranate juice

well-chilled Prosecco, to top
strip of lemon zest, to garnish

MAKES 1

Put the gin, cassis and pomegranate juice in a cocktail shaker with a handful of ice cubes and shake well. Strain into a chilled martini glass and top with Prosecco. Squeeze the lemon zest strip in half lengthways so that the essential oils in the skin spritz on to the drink, then drop it in. Serve immediately.

Festive Fizz

Fresh, fruity, fizzy and just the thing for adding seasonal sparkle to your Christmas drinks party. Cheers!

½ fresh clementine, in segments
15 ml/½ oz Cointreau
25 ml/1 oz pomegranate juice

well-chilled Prosecco, to top
pomegranate seeds, to garnish (optional)

MAKES 1

Put the clementine segments into a cocktail shaker with the Cointreau. Muddle well, then add the pomegranate juice and a handful of ice cubes and shake well. Strain into a chilled Champagne flute and add the pomegranate seeds, if using. Pour in the Prosecco and serve immediately.

Santa's Little Helper

Forget the milk and gingerbread cookies – this is what
Santa *really* wants to find when he calls at your home
this holiday season.

20 ml/¾ oz Pedro Ximenez sherry
15 ml/½ oz ginger wine
15 ml/½ oz freshly squeezed orange juice
well-chilled Prosecco, to top
strip of orange zest, to garnish
MAKES 1

Put the sherry, ginger wine and orange juice in a cocktail shaker and add
a handful of ice cubes. Shake well and strain into a chilled Champagne
flute. Top up with Prosecco. Squeeze the orange zest strip in half
lengthways so that the essential oils in the skin spritz on to the drink,
then drop it in. Serve immediately.

Index